ACTIVATING

DIVINE LOVE ENERGY

IN WATER

A WORLDWIDE HEALING SOLUTION

World Service Institute
Knoxville, Tennessee

Copyright © 2019 Robert G. Fritchie

Disclaimer: The author of this book does not dispense medical advice or prescribe the use of any medical technique as a form of treatment for physical, emotional, spiritual, or medical problems. The only intent of the author is to offer information of a nature to help in your quest for spiritual, emotional, and physical well-being.

In the event you use the information in this book for yourself, which is your constitutional right, the author, publisher, printer, and distributors assume no responsibility for your actions.

ISBN 978-0-9976905-2-1
Fritchie, Robert G.
Activating Divine Love Energy in Water
A Worldwide Healing Solution
1st edition July 2019
1. Body, Mind, Spirit - Healing - Prayer and Spiritual
2. Body, Mind, Spirit - Healing - Energy
3. Body, Mind, Spirit - Healing - General

Table of Contents

Chapter 1 Introduction 7

**Chapter 2 A Worldwide
Healing Solution 13**
Does No Harm
Sets the Mechanism to Protect
Sets the Mechanism to Receive Divine
Information
Will Help Improve Decision Making
Status of the Worldwide Healing Solution
Education Through the Worldwide Healing
Solution
Worldwide Healing Solution Objectives

**Chapter 3 You Can Help Correct
the World Health Crisis 27**
Your Role Is Important

**Chapter 4 The Energy
Principles Explained 31**
Our Spiritual Research Studies
Principle 1 - Directed Thought
Principle 2 - Divine Love
        The Love Switch

Activating Divine Love Energy in Water

Definition of Divine Love
Examples of Divine Love Healing
Principle 3 - Programmed Water
Animal Applications
Principle 4 - Resonance Transfer
About Quantum Mechanics
Experiment 1
Experiment 2
How Divine Love Energy Transfers

**Chapter 5 The Worldwide
Healing Solution Petitions 63**
First Petition
Second Petition
Expected Results
Observe Progress Reports

**Chapter 6 Development of
the Worldwide Healing Solution 71**
Sources of Poor Health
Some Illnesses Are Difficult to Treat
Approaches to Healing
Professional Fears
Attitudes
Poor Nutrition
Antibiotics Overuse
Medicinal Side Effects
Cell Damage
Health Treatment Limitations

A Worldwide Healing Solution

Contaminated Water
     Drinking Water Treatment
     The Tragedy of Waterborne Diseases
     Divine Love Heals Water
     Problems with Existing Water Treatment
     Approaches
     True Cost of Correction

**Chapter 7 Approaches
to Energy Healing 106**
Electronic Healing Devices
     Not All Devices Work
     Similar Technologies
Spiritual Approaches to Healing
North American Indian Medicine
Pure Energy Demonstrations
About Herbal Medicines
About Plants and Intention
     A True Story

**Chapter 8 Drug Addiction
and Alzheimer's Programs 127**
Drug Addiction Program
The Alzheimer's Program

**Chapter 9 Problems
Facing Humanity 133**
Many Choices, Many Problems
Meeting Health Demands

Activating Divine Love Energy in Water

Worldwide Sharing of Healthcare Treatments
Antibiotic Overuse

Chapter 10 All Living Things 144

Chapter 11 Measuring Energy 149
The Use of Dousing Wires
Build Your dousing Wires
The Principle of Dousing Wires
Using Dousing Wires
Understanding Wire Effects
Other Dousing Wire Measurements
Precautions
Practical Experiments

Chapter 1

Introduction

THIS BOOK INTRODUCES A NEW REALITY IN HEALING THAT HAS NOT BEEN USED ON A WORLDWIDE SCALE UNTIL NOW. IT PROTECTS PEOPLE FROM FURTHER DAMAGE AND FROM SIDE EFFECTS CAUSED BY HARMFUL THINGS TO WHICH THEY HAVE BEEN EXPOSED.

YOU WILL LEARN HOW TO HELP APPLY THE ENERGY OF DIVINE LOVE TO WATER SOURCES THROUGHOUT THE WORLD USING TWO SPECIAL PETITIONS.

Activating Divine Love Energy in Water

This new reality is not in conflict with religion, modern medicine, alternative medicine, or ancient medicine.

I believe that humanity has awakened to the necessity for reestablishing a spiritual connection to the Creator of the universe. We need the Creator's guidance to identify and correct some of the problems in our society and of the earth.

In this book, we address world problems with a broad spiritual solution predicated upon the joint participation and contribution of human beings, of the Angelic kingdom, and of the Creator (also known as God or the Great Spirit).

Implementing the Worldwide Healing Solution may sound like a far-fetched non-scientific approach, a challenge to organized religion, or a threat to health care practitioners, but this is definitely not the case.

A Worldwide Healing Solution

We have drawn upon 39 years of healing experience to develop and apply this new healing reality. The Solution has been developed with time-tested research described throughout the book; we explain how the Worldwide Healing Solution can complement other healing models.

This book is organized as follows:

Chapters 2 and 3 give an overview of the Worldwide Healing Solution, describing how YOU can help energetically correct world problems.

Chapters 4 and 5 provide information on how to use the Worldwide Healing Solution.

Chapter 6 explains the historical development and energetic proofs leading to a Worldwide Healing Solution.

Chapters 7 through 10 identify specific

Activating Divine Love Energy in Water

problems that we believe need to be spiritually and physically corrected throughout the world. We believe that this spiritual solution needs to be implemented immediately by working together with the energy of Divine Love.

Chapter 11 demonstrates a method to measure energy to observe the effects of the Worldwide Healing Solution.

Millions of people in the world are not likely to learn from external sources, such as books, videos, or online reference materials. Therefore, it is timely to introduce our new worldwide spiritual approach designed to protect all living things from exposure to viruses, fungi, bacteria, radiation, and chemical contamination.

The Worldwide Healing Solution is for the betterment of ALL life as people learn to apply what they are taught by the Creator.

A Worldwide Healing Solution

Let me show how YOU can help bring about the Worldwide Healing Solution reality shift to help yourself and others. Together we can eliminate many of today's problems.

Water is the Driving Force of All Nature.

~ **Leonardo da Vinci**

Chapter 2

A Worldwide
Healing Solution

The Worldwide Healing Solution is a spiritual program available to all. Other than your having a belief in a higher power, there are no preconditions or religious requirements.

We have applied our teachings in more than 35 countries having a variety of religious beliefs. Different religions may refer to Divine intelligence or a higher power by many names. In this book, we call that Divine higher power the Creator, the creative intelligence that created and maintains the universe.

The word *spiritual* is not used in the context of ghosts or parlor tricks. We define "spiritual" as a state of being in which our internal spirit guides us in every thought, word, and deed to provide whatever we need in our lives.

As guidance is received from the Creator through our intuition, we are able to perceive the spiritual truth for everything that we see, hear, smell, touch, or otherwise sense.

Over the last thirty-eight years, I have been involved in both physical and spiritual research solutions concerning spiritual energy, water, and human health.

A Worldwide Healing Solution

Four spiritual/scientific principles have emerged:

1. All people can direct energy to another person, place, or thing.

2. Throughout the universe is a powerful spiritual energy we call Divine Love.

3. Water can be "programmed" by forming a thought and directing that thought into the water using one's spiritual intention.

4. Resonance transfer is the mechanism for transferring energy from one location to another. Resonance transfer is not explained by ordinary physics but is explained with a simple application of Quantum Mechanics, which we will examine later.

The Worldwide Healing Solution Does No Harm

Our worldwide spiritual solution is not in conflict with any religion.

Our program is not in conflict with any type of medical expertise. In fact, our solution helps integrate treatment approaches for best patient outcomes, especially since we do not practice medicine.

The Worldwide Healing Solution Sets the Mechanism to Protect from Further Damage from Radiation, Poisons, Pathogens, and Chemical Agents

We cannot move into the future without accepting responsibility for our misuse of resources; we must learn to stop polluting our world.

The Worldwide Healing Solution helps avoid conditions that produce tragic out-comes by providing spiritual protection through Divine Love. This means two things:

First, our expectation is that once this spiritual solution is fully in place, human beings and all living things will be posi-tively affected. In humans, our bodies will be altered by Divine Love against further deterioration of our cellular struc-ture. Other living things will resume their intended evolution.

Second, this spiritual protection gives us time to recognize and correct things on earth that have resulted in environmen-tal poisoning of our air, land, food, and water. People who are currently ill can continue to use existing medical models or technologies and augment those modalities with Divine Love healing.

The Worldwide Healing Solution Sets the Mechanism to Receive Divine Information

Our solution provides needed information from the Creator to live a fulfilled, happy, and healthy existence. This is important because people in many nations may lack educational resources on hygiene, nutrition, medical solutions, and lifestyle changes needed for good health.

Every individual's internal spirit has the right to accept or refuse spiritual guidance from the Creator.

It is vital for everyone to be able to obtain information from within that is accurate, truthful, and without distortion.

A Worldwide Healing Solution

Gaining information from within yourself is important in the evolution of mankind. The Creator loves us and gives us the information we need, without any manipulation.

The Worldwide Healing Solution Will Help Improve Decision Making

Existing techniques and devices will continue to be used, and improved, as people switch from emotional decision-making to spiritual decision-making, based upon guidance from the Creator.

Divine Love healing is not a replacement for existing medical approaches. Yes, it can heal a variety of illnesses currently treated or not by conventional medicine. THE AT ONENESS HEALING SYSTEM ADVANCED PROTOCOL (AOHSAP) IS THE SYSTEM TO USE IF ONE IS TRYING TO CORRECT ONE'S OWN ILLNESS.

Activating Divine Love Energy in Water

(Information about the AOHSAP is found on our website.)

The fundamental goal of the Worldwide Healing Solution is not self-healing. Instead, the Program is a safeguard to prevent existing or future illnesses from attacking the body and its immune system.

We have spent many years teaching people how to incorporate divine guid-ance and Divine Love into their lives. What we have observed is that those who are willing to assume responsibility for themselves and their behavior can work with Divine Love energetically and medically to correct problems in their lives, whatever the underlying causes might be.

What has been missing in Divine Love healing is a platform for teaching people exactly what they need to change in their lives to remain well. We have tried to work with physicians in various countries to help them resolve difficult patient health problems. However, providing guidance on diet and lifestyle changes is beyond the scope of our mission.

Unless there is a sincere desire on the part of a patient to change behavior and lifestyle, healing is restricted. A given illness may be corrected with Divine Love healing, but if the patient does not change behavior as needed, the patient may develop another illness or experience a recurrence of something that has already been healed.

Perhaps science concerning cell and DNA corrections will handle future problems. However, it should be obvious that if a person's diet consists of foods containing questionable chemicals and large quantities of refined sugars, that person's health problems will likely continue. Conversely, when there is a concerted effort to improve diet and nutrition, we see that the body can achieve better health.

We also try to show people how they can operate with positive attitudes, rather than with fear, hatred, and/or despair. When Divine Love healing is incorporated with traditional medical treatment, patient outcomes are more successful and occur more quickly.

Status of the Worldwide Healing Solution

The Worldwide Healing Solution Petitions were put in place by a group of Volunteers in May 2019 for the explicit purpose of protecting people. That effort is complete.

Contaminants in water are now enshrouded with a Divine Love energy field. Now when people consume source water, Divine Love continuously protects the body from contaminants in the air, water, or food, even though some of those contaminants may still be present in a chemical analysis of the water. This is an important feature of the new reality in healing.

The Worldwide Healing Solution gives humanity an opportunity to right many of the wrongs we have perpetrated on nature and mankind.

As we begin to understand that we cannot continue to pollute our water supplies, we will be able to correct the water contaminants by actually dissolving those compounds with Divine Love. This will be done by converting the compounds into harmless ingredients.

Education Through the Worldwide Healing Solution

Education occurs through the Worldwide

Activating Divine Love Energy in Water

Healing Solution. When we ask the Creator to guide us, the Creator will lead us intuitively to the information needed to make changes in our lives. The knowledge regarding proper nutrition and other health care practices will help save lives. This connection is achieved through the second Petition of the Worldwide Healing Solution.

Worldwide Healing Solution Objectives

There are three objectives of the Worldwide Healing Solution:

1. Protect the health of human beings everywhere from further deterioration.

2. Provide information from the Creator which individuals can access intuitively to learn what they need to do.

3. Give people the time to correct their

A Worldwide Healing Solution

existing health problems with the Advanced Protocol or whatever medical approaches are available.

You may have read in my previous books how we have been able to affect positive change in persons, places, and things by working with Divine Love healing. Now you have an understanding of a new healing reality and what it does.

When someone is ill or threatened by disease, he doesn't care where a solution comes from or who gets the credit for it.

The Worldwide Healing Solution does *not* require you to:

Give up ANY treatment you are currently receiving,

Change your religious beliefs, or

Incur any expense, because the Solution is free.

Pure Water is the World's First and Foremost Medicine.

~ **Slovakian Proverb**

Chapter 3

You Can Help Correct the World Health Crisis

Your Role Is Important

You have within you the energetic power and a spiritual birthright that enables you to work with Divine Love to help yourself and mankind.

The question now becomes: *How can caring citizens, in whatever country they*

Activating Divine Love Energy in Water

live, help to eliminate physical contaminants from the water?

The answer is for YOU to help apply the Worldwide Healing Solution *using the Divine Love energy charge* available to everyone.

To help your understanding of energetic charge, consider a 1.5-volt rechargeable household battery. Such a battery cannot be recharged to higher than its intended 1.5-volt design.

A Divine Love energy charge in water has an energetic charge baseline which, although not measured in volts, operates as a battery:

Divine Love energy continuously charges to meet whatever local energy level is needed. The upper energy limit determines the extent to which a particular body of water can eliminate pollutants.

A Worldwide Healing Solution

There are two stages to the Worldwide Healing Solution.

Stage 1 - completed in May 2019 - was designed to protect all people worldwide as they later consumed their local Divine Love source water. Stage 1 also corrects local water pollution with a vibration lower than the upper vibration limit of Divine Love in that local water. This is because Divine Love can only rise to the baseline vibration level set by the total energy of the May 2019 Volunteers.

In Stage 2, as additional people say the Petitions, the baseline Divine Love contained in local source water rises to a higher baseline energy level. Eventually, the local source water can attain a vibrational energy level sufficient to physically disassociate/eliminate local source water contaminants. This is a new science.

We ask for your participation: Say the two Petitions, just once, to contribute to

Activating Divine Love Energy in Water

this humanitarian effort. Your personal spiritual Divine Love energy charge is added to the spiritual Divine Love energy of thousands of other people who have already said the Petitions.

Share the Worldwide Healing Solution with everyone you know. Let them decide for themselves if they want to help.

Chapter 4

The Energy
Principles Explained

Our Spiritual Research Studies

This chapter provides straightforward explanations of some highly technical subjects. This information is meant to help you understand additional reality applications, not dazzle you with scientific jargon.

Now let's revisit each of the four

principles in detail so that you understand how these principles emerged over time.

Principle 1 - Directed Thought

Shortly after I met Dr. Marcel Vogel, a senior material scientist with IBM, he showed me the results of an experiment he did to confirm another person's research on the effect of *thought* on a subject. Dr. Vogel had attached a philodendron plant leaf to a lie detector.

When he thought about harming the plant, the needle would deflect. When he projected a positive thought of personal love to the plant, the needle wiggled in mid-scale with minimal deviation.

This worked fine in a laboratory setting, but he wanted to know if a thought could also be directed across a significant distance and produce the same effect.

A Worldwide Healing Solution

The opportunity to test came with his trip to India, which was about 7000 miles away from California. He asked a doctor friend in San Jose, California to turn the lie detector on at specific times, once Dr. Vogel was in India.

Dr. Vogel was able to project a directed thought across space to the philodendron plant. He repeatedly demonstrated that the lie detector could measure the plant's responses to his mental intention, all in *real time*.

This monumental finding demonstrated that human beings can direct thought to a person, place, or thing, and evoke a response in the designated subject. (This experiment enabled my students to understand how we communicate with the Creator using what we call *petitions*, which are statements describing what we want to have happen.)

Dr. Vogel performed another laboratory

experiment in which he directed a thought towards a photomultiplier tube which was connected to a computer monitor. When Dr. Vogel held a thought of producing a spot of light and sending it to the tube, a point of light appeared in the middle of his blank monitor screen. Dr. Vogel was able to duplicate this effect at will.

I began to investigate this phenomenon of directed thought with groups of people gathered for the purpose of healing. We would have a client sit on a chair in the middle of a room, with ten or more volunteers sitting on chairs surrounding the client at a distance of about ten feet. The volunteers would concentrate on sending Divine Love to the client; the client would then release his/her illness using our Divine Love petitions.

Healing frequently happened during a healing session. Over many months I repeated this experiment with different individuals and got the same results.

The next step was to learn whether we could do a healing on a person at a distant location. We asked students for the name of a loved one or friend who needed healing. Then during workshops, we would each hold an intention of sending spiritual Divine Love to that recipient, who could be located in a nearby town or even thousands of miles away.

For nearby healing recipients, it was easy to get feedback/results with phone calls, but for out-of-country recipients, we encountered time delays. Results were not revealed until later when recipients could be reached.

Some reports about simple healing results tended to be subjective and not confirmed by medical tests. In the case of life-threatening diseases, we asked recipients to see their physicians and acquire any necessary test work to confirm healing.

We continued to teach the concept of directed thought over long distances in all of our workshops. People gradually realized that healing became possible because it was being Divinely given to mankind. Once they saw results based upon their own participation, they were able to accept the reality of directed thought and Divine Love healing.

Beginning in 2008, I hosted free Sunday night Internet healing webinars attended by people from more than 15 countries.

I would ask people to submit in writing what they believed they needed in the way of healing help. Then during the webinar, all of our volunteers on the webinar, wherever they were located throughout the world, would send Divine Love in real time to the individuals in need. As in live workshop sessions, the recipients would recite a Divine Love healing petition to correct their illnesses.

Now we had instant feedback because each individual healing recipient could tell the volunteers on the webinar what was happening. Some healings were completed on the webinar, especially in cases of pain. For illnesses taking longer to correct, we asked the recipient to report back on another live webinar when they received confirming results from their physicians.

Many of our dedicated volunteers attend-ed every broadcast for several years. I'm very proud of our volunteers for their selfless participation and also because many of them have also become Divine Love healing teachers.

Principle 2 - Divine Love

Divine Love is the Creator's love, which is nonjudgmental, unemotional, and unconditional.

In 1980, when I first began energy healing, I was directing my personal energy to people in need. I soon learned that this was physically draining because *my energy field would become depleted*, causing headaches and flu-like symptoms. This is NOT something you want to experience.

Because the human body stores energy like a battery, my flu-like symptoms would continue until I was able to recharge my internal battery. I learned that *when I shifted my spiritual intention from using personal love to using Divine Love, my battery (energy field) was never depleted*. Clients would also feel fully charged and much better in the presence of Divine Love.

A Worldwide Healing Solution

The Love Switch

One of the problems people have is how to know whether they are working with personal love or Divine Love. *Divine Love is a spiritual energy state*, and *personal love is a mental/physical energy state*. It is easy to switch between these two states of love, as though you had an internal switch.

When the switch is "On," you are working with Divine Love. When the switch is "Off," you are working with personal love.

If you begin a healing ceremony and you are operating without judgment, conditions or emotions, your switch is "On," and you are utilizing Divine Love.

If you try healing yourself or someone else while you are operating emotionally, have judgments or conditions that must be met by others, then your body will

Activating Divine Love Energy in Water

switch to personal love without your awareness.

You will realize you're working with personal love when you become tired and/or don't get results.

Once I understood the switching principle and tested it with a variety of clients, I began to teach it to other people in workshops. Over the years, we observed that many people operating in hostile high-stress environments would switch from Divine Love to personal love no matter what their intentions; they would then become extremely frustrated by their lack of progress.

This problem was solved with the introduction of the At Oneness Healing System Advanced Protocol, which in-cludes a provision to keep people *permanently connected to Divine Love*.

A Worldwide Healing Solution

Definition of Divine Love

When people first hear about Divine Love, some mistakenly think Divine Love is a sexual practice or is a challenge to their religious beliefs. Neither of these things is true.

The word "Divine" refers to the Creator's energy. The word "Love" refers to the Creator's unseen energy force utilized in healing.

Others have taught the principle of Divine Love as a one-way event that man cannot access except through the grace of the Creator. However, what I have found to be true is that:

Anyone who believes in the Creator can access and utilize Divine Love.

Even those who do not believe in the Creator can say the petition words, but they seldom get the desired results.

Activating Divine Love Energy in Water

Divine Love energy is a neutral energy field that exists everywhere. Neutral means that it does not exhibit a positive or a negative charge; it cannot be measured as an electrical, magnetic, or energy force *until it is activated*.

Activation of Divine Love is accomplished through Petitions. We have developed Petitions to precisely describe what we are asking the Creator to do with Divine Love. Then Divine Love responds with the frequency, intensity, and the energetic charge necessary to complete what we ask be done, according to the Creator's will.

SINCE DIVINE LOVE IS THE HIGHEST SPIRITUAL INTELLIGENCE, IT DETERMINES FOR ITSELF WHAT ATTRIBUTES ARE NEEDED, SUCH AS THE EXACT FREQUENCIES REQUIRED TO CORRECT ILLNESSES.

This is why you no longer need to apply

frequency devices and wonder whether those devices are precise, accurate, or being misapplied.

We do not use any equipment for Divine Love healing. All that is required is to hold the spiritual intention to send Divine Love to an individual, which we can do for them, or they can do for themselves, using our healing system.

We originally empowered people by teaching how to do spiritual healing as part of a group of volunteers to help others. Over the years, our programs have shifted to self-healing, where students are taught to work directly with the Creator.

In our initial healing efforts, my doctor colleagues and I developed multiple page questionnaires designed to help reveal the underlying causes of client illnesses. The data became a nightmare to interpret because cases were so complicated. Eventually, we realized that we did not have to identify the underlying causes because Divine Love manages everything.

This may be difficult to accept until you actually observe spiritual healing with Divine Love or until you receive medical reports showing your own healing progress. Some results are revealed by before and after blood analyses; others may be seen instantly by microscopic evaluation.

Testing, before and within hours after a Divine Love petition, will usually show results, e.g., that an infection has been eradicated. This is especially important to people with diseases caused by bacteria.

However, the correction of diseases caused by viruses may take longer because the damage done to the cells of the body often requires more time to heal in some cases.

A Worldwide Healing Solution

Remember:

Divine Love will automatically apply whatever energy is needed. Therefore, we don't need a clinical diagnosis, and we dont need to measure vibrational energy. All a client needs to do is describe a problem in everyday language, such as "my arm hurts," or "I feel bad."

While Divine Love healing may seem sophisticated, it is best accomplished if we just relax and let the Creator lead the way to healing. The Creator knows all about us and what is needed for us to become whole.

Our Divine Love healing results have been so profound that we began reporting what happened in several cases. You may read these reports on our website (https://www.worldserviceinstitute.org) by clicking the "Healing Reports" menu tab. These reports are in the words of the healing recipients and were published with the written permission of each.

Reading the healing reports of others has helped many clients gain the confidence needed to apply the healing principles within their own families. Everyone tends to approach Divine Love healing cautiously until personally witnessing the reality of the healing.

Examples of Divine Love Healing

To illustrate the effectiveness of Divine Love healing, I would like to share some examples of remote healing.

During the Christmas season a few years ago, a professional singer on tour in Japan telephoned asking for healing help.

Upon her arrival in Tokyo, she had developed excruciating stomach pain. She was paralyzed by the pain and could hardly move or speak. I focused on sending Divine Love while she recited a petition to release and heal her pain.

Because the pain restricted her ability to accept Divine Love, it took longer, about an hour, for her to completely recover. She was able to resume her tour the next day.

When people with severe drug addictions try on their own to stop the behavior, withdrawal symptoms result. Withdrawal can manifest as mind-numbing pain or other side effects such as nausea or an outbreak of skin sores.

I have worked with clients individually by telephone to release them from drug addictions. They were usually able to function normally within an hour or so, with no side effects, no withdrawal symptoms, and no additional emotional or physical discomfort. Within several days their bodies would rebuild, and they would be healthy with no desire to continue taking drugs. To my knowledge, none of these people have resumed a drug habit.

Principle 3 - Programmed Water

We were able to demonstrate to people in workshops that they could discharge negative thoughts into glasses of water which they held in their hands. To establish a reference point, they would taste the water before they started.

After people put their negative thoughts into the water, they found that the taste became putrid.

We also demonstrated that bad tasting water could be sweetened when we programmed the water with Divine Love.
Our *intention* should describe what the programmed water is meant to do. For

example, when we set an intention with *personal love* to increase plant growth, any plants that we watered with the programmed water produced faster growth rates than the control group.

When we used Divine Love, the growth rates were significantly higher than were attained with personal love.

I had an interesting experience with a flowering shrub in my yard. For years the shrub remained scrawny and did not bloom. One day I watered it with a Divine Love intention in the water "to make the shrub healthy." Within two weeks, the shrub began to add new growth and for the first time, bloomed with a tremendous number of flowers.

Twelve years later, that shrub continues to bloom every spring!

Animal Applications

Activating Divine Love Energy in Water

A friend had a large breed dog that had been diagnosed with cancer. I programmed a bottle of water with a Divine Love intention "to help the dog heal according to the Creator's will."

Two tablespoons of the programmed water were added to the dog's drinking water every time the water dish was refilled. Within 2 weeks, the dog seemed to be healthier. My friend then took his dog back to the veterinarian; after testing, the vet pronounced the dog to be cancer free.

Our family dog developed a growth on a hind leg which our veterinarians determined to be cancerous. Amputation of the leg was suggested to possibly correct the problem because it was likely our dog would die in a few months if the cancer spread.

We chose not to have the surgery and instead gave our dog Divine Love programmed water containing the intention "to be made well according to the Creator's will." In a few short weeks, our dog had recovered.

Principle 4 - Resonance Transfer

Resonance transfer involves moving energy from one object, such as a glass of water, to another object located at a distance.

Resonance transfer can be complicated. As soon as a glass of water is pro- grammed with Divine Love, the water will generate a Divine Love energy field in space that can be *anywhere from six inches to fifty feet*, depending upon the energy needs of the water.

This variation in measurement occurs because the Divine Love energy in the

Activating Divine Love Energy in Water

water instantly adjusts itself to meet the needs of that water.

If a second glass of water from the same source, say your tap water, is placed anywhere in the field of the first glass, the second glass of water will become charged with the same energy via resonance transfer. That second glass will generate a field in space identical to that of the first glass.

However, if the second glass of water is placed beyond the energy field of the first glass of water, resonance transfer does *not* occur in the second glass of water.

To better visualize this concept, draw a dot on a piece of paper and then draw a large circle around the dot. The dot represents the top-down view of the first glass of water. The space between the dot and the large circle denotes the Divine Love field that is generated. That field extends equidistant in all directions: above, below, and from the sides of the glass of water.

The Divine Love energy field is real and can be sensed with a variety of energy devices. Various methods are described in Chapter 11.

About Quantum Mechanics

Quantum Mechanics Theory is used to explain unexpected occurrences or test results.

Suppose we are interested in measuring a possible interaction between two materials called "A" and "B." We know from past experience that there should be three possibilities: We could see nothing but "A." Or we could see nothing but "B." Or we could see a combination of "A" and "B" together.

Activating Divine Love Energy in Water

Elementary, right?

Quantum Theory says the real outcome is selected at the time of measurement, so let's measure and see what happens.

Uh-oh... we got a different result we will call "€." We did not expect this because "C" does not include "A," "B," or a combination of those two choices.

In Quantum Mechanics, the unexpected result is explained by unseen factors that produced "C."

Now let's look at two real experiments to better understand how Quantum Mechanics explains extraordinary results.

Experiment 1

Three glasses of water were physically separated from each other by 50 feet. The first glass contained distilled water which had no chemicals in it. The second glass contained city tap water that had been run through a home reverse osmosis unit. The third glass contained city tap water containing unknown purification chemicals in it.

I programmed each glass of water independently with Divine Love to make the water safe to drink, then measured to see how far each Divine Love field projected.

The distilled water projected a Divine Love field of about 6 inches.

The reverse osmosis water projected a Divine Love field of 3 feet.

The tap water projected a Divine Love field of 20 feet.

According to Quantum Theory, several unexpected events happened:

Activating Divine Love Energy in Water

A Divine Love energy field was generated in each programmed water sample.

The energy field extended different distances in space depending upon what contaminants were in the water.

The distilled water required less energy to do precisely the same thing as the other two samples.

The reverse osmosis unit had *cleaned* up the tap water reasonably well but still required Divine Love energy to achieve the same objective.

The tap water required the most Divine Love energy.

The distance each field generated was proportional to the contamin - ation in its sample, with the most contaminated sample generating a huge Divine Love field.

These results led me to the following conclusion:

A Divine Love energy field in a body of water programmed with Divine Love increases its energy automatically to attain the energy level needed to satisfy the needs of that programmed water.

Experiment 2

I did a two-day test on my tap water using a fixed volume of 12 ounces for each sample. Each water sample was programmed with an identical Divine Love Petition shown below, and its field was then recorded. Then the sample was discarded.

Testing was done in one-hour intervals during the daytime and early evening. No

Activating Divine Love Energy in Water

samples were drawn between 10 PM and 7 AM.

The water Petition used was:

"I send Divine Love into THIS WATER SAMPLE and ask that God make the water safe for me to drink by protecting me from chemicals, viruses, harmful bacteria, radiation damage of any kind, fungi, and unbalanced stored emotions, according to God's will." (This Petition, modified slightly, became the first World-wide Healing Solution Petition.)

The results showed another unexpected event:

A succession of samples experienced a change from sample to sample. The Divine Love field increased slowly from 22 to 28 feet on Day 1. During Day 2, the field slowly returned to 22 feet.

A Worldwide Healing Solution

I wondered why the number jumped so high until I realized that we were experiencing a progressive deterioration in our water supply accompanied by a strong odor of chlorination during the first day. Also, weather conditions on Day 1 had been unsettled with temperatures in the high 80s, an air pollution warning, and a severe thunderstorm.

This demonstrated that the Divine Love energy fields in the individual samples drawn from my municipal tap water, expanded on Day 1 to meet the increase in environmental contamination and then decreased to "normal" on Day 2.

Could there have been a different contamination source, say from an industrial spill? That may be a possibility, but it does not change the significance of what happened to the sample energy fields.

How does this theory apply to Divine Love programmed water in nature?

How Divine Love Energy Transfers

If you programmed a small bucket of ordinary water with the two Worldwide Healing Solution Petitions, that bucket of water would accept your Petitions and behave like the glasses of water in Experiment 1.

You could then accurately measure the distance the Divine Love field generates from your bucket of water.

If you then placed your bucket of water next to a small pond, the bucket water's Divine Love energy would be resonance transferred into the pond.

The pond's Divine Love energy would immediately increase to meet the needs of the pond. Note that I said the energy in the pond increased.

A Worldwide Healing Solution

You could measure the field generated from the pond alone by completely removing the bucket from the area.

If the pond has an outlet to a brook, the pond's Divine Love energy will in turn immediately be resonance transferred to the entire brook. The brook will then adjust its own Divine Love field up or down.

If the brook empties into a river, that river will also become energetically charged by resonance transfer from the pond. Then the river will immediately increase its Divine Love field to meet the needs of the entire river.

This is how resonance transfer can be used for connected bodies of water.

I've explained how Divine Love energy is resonance transferred to any body of water. It is important to understand how

Activating Divine Love Energy in Water

each water source adjusts to its own energy needs.

Divine Love will not allow a water supply to remain contaminated or poisoned.

Chapter 5

The Worldwide Healing Solution Petitions

Each of us is a spiritual being with a human body. One's age, sex, race, nationality, or religion are unimportant. Our core beliefs are also irrelevant because they may be based upon inaccurate information passed down from previous generations.

We need to trust that the Creator will

provide direction when we ask for help. Each of us has at least two Guardian Angels that work to help and guide us. In addition, many of the Creator's Angels serve throughout the world to help guide people.

Following are two simple petitions that you SAY ONLY ONE TIME EACH. When you say the Petitions, your Divine Love energy is added to the energy of all people and Angels who are participating in this spiritual program. All of the petitions combine and are stored in water systems everywhere.

First Petition

Please do not change the wording. Say aloud just once:

"I ask that all the angels help implement this petition. We send Divine Love into every water source and ask that God make that water safe for people to drink by protecting all people and life forms from chemicals, viruses, harmful bacteria, radiation damage of any kind, fungi, and unbalanced stored emotions, according to God's will."

Once you have said this petition, draw in your breath with your mouth closed and then pulse your breath with your mouth closed as if you were trying to clear your nose. Pulsing breath releases your Divine Love energy petition into water everywhere.

Your Divine Love energy is added to the Divine Love energy of thousands of other people who have said this same petition.

Second Petition

The second petition is intended to provide the knowledge base that people need to become and stay healthy. This is

Activating Divine Love Energy in Water

necessary because health education is deficient in many places.

Please do not change the wording of this petition. Say aloud just once:

"I ask that all the angels help implement this petition. We send Divine Love into every water source and ask that God provide each human being with whatever knowledge they need to understand and apply the energy, nutrition, foods, medicines, and herbs needed to attain and maintain their health."

To release the energy petition, draw in your breath with your mouth closed and then pulse your breath with your mouth closed as if you were trying to clear your nose.

Note: The information presented in my other books has evolved from group healing into individualized healing, com- monly called "self-healing." We have taught people to think in terms of what they physically feel, such as pain or anxiety, because it is through a physical or emotional feeling that the body alerts us when something is wrong.

All of our teachings have been distilled into two reference documents from which you can learn how to implement your own self-healing using our At Oneness Healing System Advanced Protocol.

The first reference is the book DYNAMIC REALITIES AND DIVINE LOVE HEALING; the second reference is the ADVANCED PROTOCOL AND HEALING STATEMENT TRAINING VIDEO. Both of these references can be found through our website at https://www.worldserviceinstitute.org. Thousands of people have applied our reference material to effect healing in their own bodies.

Expected Results

As we consume Divine Love energy drinking water, our systems will begin an energetic conversion process to protect us from further deterioration from existing illnesses AND from new diseases for which there are no current treatments. These changes become effective when the energy field of the local water reaches the energy level needed to manifest local changes.

Continue to use the At Oneness Healing System Advanced Protocol to correct most existing illnesses. Just remember that Divine Love can change anything if the Creator wills it.

Observe Progress Reports

Watch for:

A Worldwide Healing Solution

Reductions in international water borne illnesses.

Evidence of unexplained reductions in international infectious diseases as reported in the world's scientific and government publications.

Reports of spontaneous individual healing of specific illnesses.

Unexplained improvements in general human health issues as reported in the press.

Improvements in your own health and that of your family. Remember that if you have a serious disease, the Worldwide Healing Solution is designed to stabilize, but not necessarily heal, your disease.

It is up to you to make life changes and apply the At Oneness Healing System Advanced Protocol and other modalities

Activating Divine Love Energy in Water

you can access to heal your existing
problem.

Chapter 6

Development of the Worldwide Healing Solution

My professional work experience includes solving complex technical problems in industrial and municipal water treatment plants.

In 1979, I began a personal quest to discover ways to help people. Little did I realize that decision would lead me to

71

Activating Divine Love Energy in Water

learn about entirely new realities and methods of healing.

My friendship with Dr. Marcel Vogel, a senior material scientist with IBM, enabled me to learn about the energy of the human body and the application of Divine Love healing.

Marcel and I taught energy healing workshops during which we were able to demonstrate how to correct a variety of illnesses. It did not matter what the illnesses were; most people responded to healing.

We eventually learned that the root cause of a problem could be addressed in spiritual healing without the need to actually identify that root cause, or where it originated. This has helped many clients to stop obsessing about the causes of their illnesses.

In those early years of healing work, I

realized that what we were doing was Divinely guided because there was no logic to explain how someone could heal from, for example, a stage IV cancer, achieving complete wellness, sometimes in less than a month.

Through spiritual healing research, those four fundamental Principles (see Chapter 4) emerged, clarifying how energy can be applied to human beings to produce healing results. Those Principles are presented and discussed in this book to help you understand the reality of what has become known as Divine Love Healing and its relationship to the World-wide Healing Solution.

People have both complimented and criticized my healing work. The compli-ments were from people who learned to apply the principles and recover their health. The criticisms were levied by people who considered my efforts too different from their own concepts of reality and/or denied the principles being taught, which ultimately restricted their own healing.

It became apparent that once people learned the fundamental Principles, they got results that usually improved their lives. And, once they took responsibility for the healing process, they also learned that Divine Love healing complemented whatever other healing modalities they used.

Sources of Poor Health

Today we know that our health can be adversely affected by a variety of things. We will examine three broad causes of illness:

1. Environmental Chemical Poisoning from the Air We Breathe, the Foods We Eat, and Substances We Absorb Through the Skin.

A Worldwide Healing Solution

Almost everything we come into contact with is suspect. When we shop, few of us read product labels to learn what is in our products. And when we find a list of unknown ingredients, we are not always able to evaluate the product's potential damage to our health.

Many of the compounds we consume or put on our skin, pass into our organs and bloodstream. As these toxins build up in our systems, we may reach a point such that our bodies cannot clear toxins fast enough to maintain our health.

Brain damage is becoming more prevalent from contact sports and from various combat-induced stress disorders.

A newly diagnosed brain disorder called Frontotemporal Dementia (FTD) attacks younger adults, causing them to lose awareness of who they are and what they are saying. This disorder has no cure and usually results in death within 2 to 5 years. A medical team in Los Angeles has been making a great effort, analyzing brain scans, and looking for potential treatments. This may be a situation where we do need to understand the root cause of this brain damage effect.

For example, if scientists can identify that the root cause of a health problem is a particular food, people may be able to physically avoid that food, which would lessen the number of cases. We have not yet had the opportunity to apply Divine Love healing to FTD but welcome anyone who asks for help.

2. Emotional Damage That We Energetically Hold Onto.

Our thoughts and emotions are really energy clusters. Over time, emotional energy clusters interfere with cell health, resulting in a compromised immune system. Then one is subject to illnesses that a healthy immune system would ordinarily correct.

Stored emotions include both suppressed and subconscious feelings. We also need to learn to forgive ourselves and others.

3. Radiation Damage from X-Rays, Electronic Equipment, and Nuclear and Cosmic Energy.

For many years, scientists have known about damage from excessive *X-Rays*. Some researchers also report that other widely used medical diagnostic equipment can produce cumulative radiation damage.

Proximity to electronic equipment can expose us to potential damage from escaping electromagnetic energy. This hot topic is the subject of studies worldwide. For example, recent scientific publications have reported that the brains of young children are affected by electromagnetic interference when the children spend too much time wearing or holding electronic devices. However, if the exposure is not prolonged, it appears that the brain can recover in a few hours.

This suggests that brain damage is a function of both the radiation level and the duration of repeated exposure to specific electronic devices. No one really understands the long-term detrimental effects.

Nuclear radiation is a significant problem. The 1986 atomic event at the Chernobyl Nuclear Power Plant in Ukraine (formerly part of the Soviet Union) resulted in many deaths from radiation sickness and cancer.

However, the Fukushima, Japan, disaster in 2011 does not have a record of deaths attributable to nuclear radiation damage. Doctors there are very conservative but have *not* seen the outbreak of cancers or

78

other radiation illnesses expected for the radiation levels emitted.

When the Fukushima reactor damage was first announced, we performed a group healing with 551 Volunteers with the intention to protect the people of Japan and all life. *This is an alternate reality because Divine Love healing was used to help prevent the materialization of widespread nuclear illness.*

I hope that scientists will eventually recognize that radiation damage can be corrected using our healing process. As scientists engage in Divine Love applications, they will quickly learn that results cannot be explained by conventional physics, but can be understood by Quantum Mechanics (Quantum Physics), briefly described in Chapter 4. Cosmic radiation damage is a subject of major scientific investigation in both the private sector and by governments.

Activating Divine Love Energy in Water

The Van Allen Belts, which were discovered in 1958, are comprised of two levels of radiation belts held in place by the energy field of the Earth. The inner belt is made up of protons, and the outer belt is made up of electrons. The belts begin about 400 miles above Earth and extend into deep space.

When the space program began, there were concerns the astronauts would be adversely affected by their experiences. NASA calculated the astronauts would receive a minimum dose of radiation for the one hour it took for them to pass through the Van Allen Belts on the way to the moon. Anyone staying in the middle of these radiation belts for an extended period would receive a lethal dose of cosmic radiation.

We are also subjected to the energy of the sun's solar flares, another form of cosmic radiation. High levels of cosmic radiation from deep space are much more damaging than solar flares from the sun. This is because some of the star systems have much higher radiation levels than the sun has. It remains to be seen whether deep space cosmic radiation is increasing.

Scientists know there are two types of cosmic rays. One passes through all matter and reaches Earth. The other can be partially deflected from Earth.

When radiation storms from solar flares are expected, astronauts protect themselves by sheltering in shielded areas installed on the space station. I have also been told that there have been instances when astronauts were physically removed from the space station. This was done to avoid cumulative radiation damage when prolonged radiation bursts were expected. Cosmic rays are known to be cancer-causing.

Activating Divine Love Energy in Water

The U.S. astronaut Scott Kelly was on the International Space Station for 342 days beginning in March 2015. Researchers discovered that his genes were affected by the space flight, with changes to his immune system; Kelly's mental abilities also declined. Kelly was exposed to high levels of cosmic radiation; this can result in long-term health effects such as cancer.

There are no medical treatments capable of reversing the type of damage that astronauts encounter except for the application of Divine Love healing.

Several years ago, I learned of an increase in cosmic rays sweeping across the Earth like a giant paintbrush. I borrowed equipment to measure the radiation and observed days when the device registered high bursts of cosmic radiation. The radiation bursts were rapid, causing the instrument needle to jump back and forth.

A Worldwide Healing Solution

Obviously, everyone and everything on Earth would also be receiving these cosmic rays.

The scientific debate continues as to whether global warming is causing the ice fields to recede. There are other possibilities: For example, if scientists learn that cosmic rays occur more frequently at the North and South Poles, then an argument can be advanced that cosmic ray energy may be partially responsible for melting polar ice.

We have strong evidence that Divine Love healing can correct nuclear and electromagnetic damage. I expect that cosmic radiation effects can be dealt with effectively by Divine Love, in both spiritual healing and prevention of further damage, using the Worldwide Healing Solution.

Some Illnesses
Are Difficult to Treat

Bacterial problems are discussed in Chapter 9.

Fungi that lie dormant in our systems are activated when we are out of balance energetically. Fungi are correctable through Divine Love healing.

Viruses include the flu, chicken pox, and cold sores. Because the flu virus mutates quickly, protection through vaccination is complicated. This year's vaccine is based upon last year's flu strain, and it takes months to manufacture sufficient supply to meet demand. That is why, even if you've had a flu shot this year, the protection you receive may not prevent the flu.

Response to the threat of other virulent virus strains has both health and financial considerations.

A Worldwide Healing Solution

It can be challenging to allocate research, manufacturing, and in-field resources to stop limited virus threats. Viruses are responsible for severe illnesses such as AIDS and Ebola, for which there are no "one-shot" medicinal solutions. Suppressing virus outbreaks is a key objective of the Worldwide Healing Solution.

Approaches to Healing

Divine Love healing alone may not be enough; information about nutrition, the correct use of herbal and food supplements, and being able to release uncontrolled emotions are all important to achieve permanent healing.

We also need to recognize and eliminate other limitations to healing:

Activating Divine Love Energy in Water

Professional Fears

Some physicians believe that if Divine Love energy becomes the norm for healing, that they will be out of business. This is limited thinking for several reasons.

First of all, although invention originates with the Creator, physicians are necessary to work with these inventions. We may develop medicines, equipment, and techniques to help people, but we must do so in a responsible manner, without causing harm.

Secondly, we need to accept that we are all spiritual human beings, not just creatures of nature seeking spirituality. Once we understand that we are spiritual beings, we can communicate with the Creator, ask the Creator for help, and accept the Creator's energy as needed to correct problems.

A Worldwide Healing Solution

Realize that the Creator's energy is Divine Love and that Divine Love is the most powerful healing force in the universe.

Attitudes

While many people anxiously seek improvements in their health, they do not understand the need to change negative attitudes and feelings of hopelessness into positive attitudes full of hope.

This transition in attitude is critical because what you think concerning yourself and others affects your body's energy and wellness.

Those who have been abused and/or suffer from low self-esteem need to make permanent adjustments in lifestyle and not continue to live in unhealthy environments.

Activating Divine Love Energy in Water

Our At Oneness Healing System Advanced Protocol teaches people how to work successfully with Divine Love.Those who fully engage and take responsibility for their health are usually able to break free from toxic environments.

This negative attitude problem is addressed in Petition 2 of our Worldwide Healing Solution.

Poor Nutrition

Since the mid-1960s, increasingly poor dietary practices have weakened our immune systems; correcting the resulting poor health is a complex problem.

It is essential that we learn the importance of a nutritious diet. A poor diet containing excessive amounts of salt and refined sugar, so-called "bad" carbohydrates, and synthetic food preservatives can create many health problems.

A Worldwide Healing Solution

Nutrition information is provided through the Worldwide Healing Solution.

Antibiotics Overuse

When we misuse or overuse medicines, those medicines can become ineffective or poisonous to our systems. Antibiotics have often been prescribed too frequently or unnecessarily. Essential antibiotics such as penicillin may no longer be effective for people who have frequently used antibiotics throughout their lives. This problem is addressed in more detail in Chapter 9.

Medicinal Side Effects

It is virtually impossible to anticipate all of the potential side effects of medicines. I believe this is because a new medication can interact with previously ingested drugs or other toxins that may be stored in the body. These interactions can produce harmful side effects in both the short-term and long-term.

In my experience, people exhibiting harmful side effects respond well to Divine Love Healing. Perhaps the best way for medication manufacturers to limit product side effects is to ask for and apply the Creator's Divine guidance during the product development phase.

In our new Worldwide Healing Solution, the objective is to protect people from further deterioration of their health. This does not mean that all individual illness is healed immediately. It does mean that each individual is stabilized, so that side effects do not manifest. This is an excellent example of how science and Divine Love spiritual healing can complement one another.

Cell Damage

The underlying causes of some illnesses are known and explained in terms of new sciences such as epigenetics (how biological systems switch genes on and off) and DNA damage correction (usually caused by chemical/radiation damage). Researchers are also learning how genes improve as one's emotions are managed.

Stem cell therapy, also known as regenerative medicine, is the use of stem cells to treat or prevent a disease or condition. This technology can be time-intensive, costly, and not available to everyone.

Insurance companies may be reluctant to underwrite some medical procedures until they can be shown to be more cost-effective.

Many emerging infectious diseases throughout the world have limited treatment options; healthcare resources are also spread too thin. Some countries and many rural sections of the United States have too few qualified physicians and struggle to provide even basic medical services.

The preceding are examples of problems that we are unable to easily resolve. However, we have seen many cases of cell repair occurring with Divine Love healing.

I expect that our new Worldwide Healing Solution will help lessen stress in areas where it is needed most. By preventing the immune system from becoming weakened and protecting against disease by using the energy of Divine Love, we should see a reduction in outbreaks both in the USA and abroad.

Health Treatment Limitations

Many professional physicians have dedi-cated their lives to serving the public, and in most cases, they have been successful. However, doctors, care providers, and others in the healing arts often fail to share information among themselves and also do not offer integrated solutions to their patients or to their clients.

For example, proper nutrition and the use of herbal remedies can help restore and build robust immune systems. A healthy immune system is capable of reversing many illnesses.

Yet while health experts try to educate the public on what to do, and what not to do, cases of obesity, cancer, diabetes, and heart disease continue to increase. Medical schools do not offer enough nutrition education and existing knowledge is not being well or widely distributed.

I do not believe that a diagnosis of cancer necessarily means a person is going to die if they do not immediately embrace aggressive treatment. A cancer diagnosis is frightening, but we know that cancer does not manifest overnight.

Activating Divine Love Energy in Water

Cancer can develop over 5 to 10 years (or more) and have many causes.

Sometimes cancer is caused by underlying negative emotions that need to be energetically released to achieve successful healing. Other causes include poor diets, radiation, and environmental toxins. Once an unhealthy practice or unhealthy environment is identified as a cause of cancer, it is important to correct the situation.

In the United States, cancer is often treated aggressively with chemotherapy, radiation, or surgery. In Asia, many doctors take a less aggressive approach and focus instead on improving overall health without specifically trying to target cancer. There is scientific evidence that some cancers can be treated with a wide assortment of herbal and nutritional approaches that do not introduce harmful side effects.

A Worldwide Healing Solution

Some Chinese and Indian herbs target cancer cells quite effectively. In some cases, cancer cells remain but are no longer life-threatening. Thus, many cancer patients can have longer lives.

Some researchers have been able to penetrate the outer wall of cancer stem cells with intravenous vitamins and herbal solutions that starve the cancer cells. The cancer cells then die. These practices and technologies should be more readily shared throughout the world.

I believe successful healing regimens should not be available only to those who can afford expensive solutions, or to those who have health insurance coverage. Instead, we need a more universal approach, where less costly solutions, together with Divine Love healing, can be implemented, particularly in areas with limited medical resources.

Activating Divine Love Energy in Water

Years ago, as I pondered ways to solve this health integration problem, I realized that a Divine Love spiritual solution does not conflict with ongoing medical research. Divine Love healing can help focus all efforts into a more cohesive approach toward healing.

The universal guidance of our spiritual solution will help correctly apply what the Creator has provided us through nature, medicine, and technology.

Contaminated Water

Millions of people throughout the world do not have safe drinking water. In developed nations, municipal water treatment systems attempt to correct an assortment of chemical contaminants and pathogens.

However, many modern-day chemicals entering surface water are difficult to

A Worldwide Healing Solution

remove from drinking water. As these contaminants continue to accrue, we could be facing a potential health time bomb.

Drinking Water Treatment

Many places in the world have inadequate sanitation and/or heavily polluted water. Often people throughout the affected regions drink contaminated water without even boiling the water to purify it.

Some countries are dependent upon charitable organizations to provide safe drinking water via bottled water or newly dug wells, or improved sanitation practices. Portable devices capable of purifying drinking water, including water purification tablets and solar powered distillation, may also be used. However, much of this technology is not available to millions of people.

Activating Divine Love Energy in Water

Increased flooding in the years 2017-2019 has introduced pollution hazards in commercial water plants in the United States, the European Union, Australia, and other countries. These floods impede efforts to maintain healthy drinking water sources.

There is also an influx of contaminants from manufacturing enterprises. These contaminants, once they are identified in drinking water, often require special handling and additional costly treatment processes.

The existing technology available to these plants includes:

Activated carbon particles that adsorb many chemicals.

Large-scale reverse osmosis units to treat specific chemicals or toxins such as lead.

A Worldwide Healing Solution

A family of industrial chemicals to bind certain pollutants in water and precipitate them in settling basins.

Industrial biochemical oxygen-demand plants using live bacteria to eat sophisticated toxic chemicals.

Why is this technical information important? Because, even when sophisticated technologies are used, there are indications that trace quantities of toxic chemicals remain in the water. Those chemicals can accumulate in human tissue and become a problem as we age.

The Tragedy of Waterborne Diseases

Waterborne diseases, such as the 2019 cholera outbreaks in Mozambique, are a huge problem. Cholera is a bacterial disease that causes rapid dehydration through diarrhea; if not treated promptly, cholera can lead to death within hours. Treatments are re-hydration and inoculations where possible; however, these remediation programs may not be able to keep up with sudden demand when there are outbreaks of this deadly infectious disease.

A report by Reuters on April 3, 2019, indicated that agencies such as The World Health Organization require funding far greater than the funds currently available, just to deal with the cholera outbreak in Mozambique.

This is another example of the need to implement a Worldwide Healing Solution.

Divine Love Heals Water

Case 1-Healing Water:

A few years ago there was extensive rainfall in parts of North Carolina, where there are many pig farms. There was great concern that sewage from the

A Worldwide Healing Solution

flooded pig farms would reach and con-
taminate local surface water and wells.

At the urging of a volunteer in a healing
group, we performed a healing ceremony, with the help of the Angelic kingdom,
to prevent harm to human life.

*Despite extensive flooding, the expected
health hazard did not materialize.*

Case 2- Healing Water:

Before the Katrina hurricane of 2011,
New Orleans officials were concerned
that with any flooding, the extremely
polluted Lake Pontchartrain would introduce many health problems.

We performed a healing ceremony with
one of our healing groups, utilizing
Divine Love petitions, intended to protect
all the people and animals of New
Orleans from contaminated flood water.

Activating Divine Love Energy in Water

The flooding was severe. I personally saw the high water flood marks in downtown New Orleans; where I stood had been 12 feet underwater!

Yet, there were no reported outbreaks of waterborne chemical contaminants or pathogens affecting human beings.

People thought that the flooding helped decrease pollution in Lake Pontchartrain sufficiently to warrant reopening the beaches for swimming. Those same beaches had been closed for many years because of existing contamination.

Could a water flush alone correct all those problems? I find it interesting that the public does not always recognize a miracle!

These two case examples should give you a sense of the new reality of world healing that we are introducing in this book.

A Worldwide Healing Solution

Problems with Existing Water Treatment Approaches

Chemicals like polychlorinated biphenyls, chlorine dioxide, and dioxins have entered the water in various locations. These contaminants are currently being partially extracted from drinking water using carbon adsorption where such equipment is installed. However, the extraction is only about 86% effective, so these pollutants are still affecting some water supplies.

Water dilution has been used to reduce toxin concentrations to supposedly safe levels, but the cumulative toxic effects of multiple contaminants are difficult to identify and treat. The potential exists for cumulative toxicity in the human body.

The improper disposal of pharmaceutical drugs and industrial grade solvents introduces additional health hazards with unknown long-term effects.

True Cost of Correction

Engineers design facilities using best practices and the best technology. Yet few designers can anticipate all potential or probable events. Many water plants in the United States and other countries are aging, operating well beyond their original design lives. When a disaster creates contaminated flood waters, and toxic materials are present, health concerns are paramount. Remediation, however, can exceed the treatment capabilities of water plants. Associated costs most of remediation usually exceed available budgets.

Plants may add new processes to deal with problems. For example, a plant might consider commercial reverse osmosis (RO) to remove large molecules such as lead from water. However, reverse osmosis does not remove volatile organic chemicals, pesticides, and solvents. Therefore a plant may need to

A Worldwide Healing Solution

install even more costly hybrid solutions.

There will always be new sources of contaminants presented which may go undetected, untested and/or untreated. The new reality in the Worldwide Healing Solution offers an alternative way to protect people.

Chapter 7

Approaches to Energy Healing

In the 1960s, Italian scientists reported the discovery of positive electrical charges on the surface of human organs. Think of these charges as protective electrical shields around every organ, every nerve, every muscle, and every bone.

The researchers reported that when a negatively charged invasive molecule comes into contact with a positive charge located on the protective electrical shield of an organ, the negatively-charged molecule strips away the positive charge on the organ. This provides an entry point for further invasion of the organ by negatively charged molecules.

Note: Cells are attacked by negative charges, which can eventually cause cells to mutate or die as they succumb to invading disease molecules.

Electronic Healing Devices

Other countries have developed novel approaches to correct "electronic" deficiencies in the human body.

For example:

Researchers learned that every illness, be it viral, bacterial, or parasitic, has its own distinctive vibration level called a

Activating Divine Love Energy in Water

"frequency." Several machines developed in Europe measure the frequency of an illness, but learning what to do with that frequency took several years.

All of us have seen a symmetrical sine wave curve. In electronics, alternating current is represented by a sine wave that starts at a zero point, rises to a peak over time, then slopes downward and goes below the horizontal starting point to the wave's lowest point. Then the curve starts upward again, continuing to the right. See the diagram below.

Let's simplify by saying that every illness has its own sine-like wave; the highest point of the sine wave represents the frequency at which a given illness is at maximum strength. The lowest point of the sine wave represents the lowest frequency of an illness, below which the specific illness doesn't exist.

A Worldwide Healing Solution

If a researcher can find the exact frequency emitted by an illness, he can usually apply the inverse of that frequency to neutralize the illness. Interestingly, different machines have produced the same results.

I evaluated several of these electronic machines in the 1980s as part of a spiritual research project. The fundamental problem with these devices was that precision errors in the measuring equipment often produced frequencies that were slightly different than what was needed for healing.

This measurement variance hindered healing and produced incomplete results or no results at all. However, as electronic component technology has advanced, the precision of the devices has been improved.

Similar equipment available today from Europe is much more precise and yields better results, but such instrumentation is not universally approved for use, particularly in the United States.

Not All Devices Work

I recall being in Oakland, California, for a meeting with a group of medical doctors. One of the doctors had just received a new machine from Europe that he wanted help evaluating.

A book of illness frequencies came with the device. A patient would hold a probe in each hand, the machine would be turned on, and the doctor would read the patient's operating frequency on a meter built into the device.

Then the doctor would consult his book to determine if an illness was present at the operating frequency of the patient. If present, the precise frequency setting to neutralize the illness was sent through the probes into the patient's body.

110

A Worldwide Healing Solution

My intuition told me that this device was unreliable, so I asked the doctor what the reading would be for cancer and he gave me a number. I held the probes, and without telling him, I thought of the exact numeric value he provided me.

Then, I asked him to turn on the device. When he did, he stepped back in alarm when the machine registered the cancer number he had just given me.

He had unknowingly purchased a device that interacted with the energy field of the mind.

Next, I asked how quickly he expected to see results when he was providing treatment. He told me that after a week of several treatments, the objective was to reach a zero reading on the instrument. While the machine was on, I held the thought of a zero reading. Amazingly, the instrument needle dropped immediately to zero!

Activating Divine Love Energy in Water

The doctor was visibly upset when I told him what I had been doing. We repeated the test using the frequency number for a blood illness.

This time I told him what I was doing as I thought about the number. When he measured me, he saw a reading corresponding to a blood illness problem. Then, I held the thought that my blood was normal, and the reading fell to zero.

When I asked the doctor for his opinion on the device, he responded by picking it up, and dropping the entire system into his trash receptacle!

The point of this true story is to remind you that human beings are not just physical specimens. Each of us has a three-component connection, which is your inner spirit, your mind, and your physical body.

When you are in balance electrically and

A Worldwide Healing Solution

working with your *spirit* rather than your *mind*, you can change measurable conditions in your physical body. I have repeatedly demonstrated this by controlling my blood pressure and pulse rate.

This emphasizes the point that *with spirit and Divine Love, we <u>can</u> change ourselves.*

Working devices have been developed and are accepted in several European countries. Similarly, several Far Eastern countries with very liberal laws regarding the application of medicines, herbs, and electronic devices allow doctors to apply whatever is in their patient's best interest. Most of the modern diagnostic or treatment electronic devices used in the Far East have been imported from Europe. China and Russia have also developed electronic devices to treat illness.

Similar Technologies

Laboratory research involving microscopic examination is usually conducted using nonliving specimens.

There is a resurgence of interest in what is called "dark field microscopy," which uses live specimens and light sources that do not influence the samples. A researcher observes through his microscope as he experiments with frequencies intended to destroy live specimens.

The best-known device was initially developed in the United States by Roger Rife, who perfected a system to kill live cancer specimens. Once he had identified the correct frequency, he was able to send that frequency to patients and reportedly, successfully eradicated some cancers.

Several doctors initially endorsed Rife's technology but later withdrew support because of the threat the technology represented to traditional medicine.

Western medicine is focused on patented drugs for treatment, and can be closed-minded about other technologies. Dark field microscopy continues to be banned in the United States, but does well else-where, with devices similar to Rife's.

Spiritual Approaches to Healing

We normally think in terms of three dimensions, based upon what we can physically see. Spiritual energy, however, is not seen with the naked eye and has its origin in a fourth dimension. I want to familiarize you now with several different healing approaches that employ unseen frequencies in a different manner.

A holy man in India draws a picture of a lotus flower on paper, and then assigns healing energy for a specific illness to each petal or part of the flower. When he gives the physical drawing to a patient, the patient places a container of drinking water directly on the drawing. The frequency (energy) associated with the picture is transferred into the water. The resulting energized water is consumed by the patient to successfully treat a specific illness!

In Japan, Emoto demonstrated a similar energy effect. Using polluted water from Tokyo Bay, he filled two glass jars: one jar for the test and one jar for the control sample. Then he drew a love symbol on a piece of paper and taped it to the outside of the test jar. Emoto next put a few drops of water from the test jar onto a slide; he put a few drops of water from the control jar onto another slide. Both slides were then put into a freezer.

Mr. Emoto found that the energy of personal love transferred from the love symbol into the water as evidenced by beautiful hexagonal, snowflake-like, crystalline formations in the frozen water drops. In contrast, the slide with the polluted water sample from the control jar showed ugly striations and no symmetry. Emoto published several books describing these experiments and the effect of his personal love intentions mentally projected into water.

I expanded on the experiments of India and Japan by programming water with the higher spiritual energy of Divine Love rather than personal love energy. As described earlier in Chapter 4, Principle 4, when Divine Love is projected into water, it generates a large energy field capable of healing.

North American Indian Medicine

North American medicine chiefs acknowledge healing energy as coming from the

Activating Divine Love Energy in Water

Great Spirit (Creator). Most use it in their ceremonies and practices.

Their energy techniques are often applied to drinking water containing a programmed intention to help a person. This is usually done as part of a sweat lodge ceremony where someone is being purged of toxins by sweating profusely.

In the mid-1980s a man I knew as Grandfather was the Medicine Chief of the Chumash Indians in California.

Grandfather was concerned that the spiritual healing practices of his people were being forgotten in our present-day society. He shared much of his knowledge and exposed me to many Indian practices.

The reality is that Indian medicine is very spiritual and effective.

Pure Energy Demonstrations

One weekend Marcel Vogel was invited to lecture at the Esalen Institute in Big Sur, California. After Marcel asked me to accompany him, I was inspired to pack my Indian drum and an orange cloth, although I had no specific plan to use them.

The next morning a group of psychiatrists and psychologists assembled for our lecture on the lawn of Esalen Institute. Marcel was accustomed to presenting facts based on upon scientific experimentation, allowing people time to gradually absorb information.

When Marcel began to speak about the spiritual nature of healing and its importance, I noticed that all but one doctor in the group had essentially "tuned out" his lecture.

Activating Divine Love Energy in Water

When it was my turn to speak, I wanted to give the group a wake-up call. Since drumming is widely used in ceremonies throughout the world, I decided to do a demonstration.

There are specific drum beats that, when done in conjunction with intention, affect material things.

I asked the doctor who had listened to Marcel attentively to help, positioning her about ten feet in front of the others. She was to hold the drum with the flat side facing the doctors, who were standing in a group. I demonstrated to her the beat I wanted her to apply, and she started to beat the drum.

I withdrew about twenty feet from her on the opposite side of the drum, furthest from the group. Then I projected through the drum the thought of physically moving the doctors.

A Worldwide Healing Solution

Immediately, they all staggered backward; some even sat down suddenly on the ground. The astonished doctors were beginning to understand that there are spiritual energy forces that cannot be seen with the naked eye.

Because the doctors were still not entirely convinced of this reality, I gave them another demonstration I learned from a Tibetan monk.

Monks wear orange garments for a particular reason: when energy passes through an orange garment, it enables energy to act on an intention.

I asked the woman doctor to hold up my orange cloth with the flat side facing the doctors. This time I asked the doctors to stand in a single line facing the orange cloth. Each doctor put his hands on the shoulders of the person ahead of him. I asked them to brace their feet so that they were in a strong defensive posture-

one foot slightly ahead of the other with the upper body leaning forward.

I pulsed my breath toward the orange cloth while holding an intention to move the doctors. This time they all fell to the ground, totally shocked. Ordinarily, it would take a very strong person to move twenty-five people.

After lunch, when Marcel resumed teaching, his audience had gone through a significant spiritual awakening and was now most attentive. This was evidenced by the insightful questions asked and their interest in further study of energy healing.

About Herbal Medicines

Countries such as China, India Thailand, Indonesia, and the Philippines, often use available natural herbs and other plant products to correct many illnesses and diseases naturally.

Medicine chiefs and shamans regularly harvest and use herbs and plants in the Americas and other countries. Some open-minded medical researchers are interacting with shamans to learn what plants and herbs can be used for treating illness. And doctors have been publishing articles in scientific journals documenting how the cellular structure in humans is affected by the use of herbal medicines.

For many in the world who cannot afford the most advanced traditional medical solutions, herbal medicine offers a viable alternative.

About Plants and Intention

In nature, many plants provided by the Creator are both a food source and contain energy frequencies needed to correct particular illnesses. These plants are not the same as herbs, which are used in smaller quantities.

Also, some plants are not assigned by the Creator to provide particular functions for human beings; this is where intention plays a significant role. A shaman can use a spiritual intention to program individual plants to assist in correcting an illness by specifying a function to be performed.

When using certain devices, one must specify exact frequencies. But this is not necessary when you accept that you can use Divine Love and your spiritual intention. You link directly to the Creator, receive information you need intuitively, and the correct frequencies for what you are trying to achieve are automatically applied.

I believe shamans and medicine chiefs to be closely linked to the Creator; they should be respected and honored.

A True Story

One summer, our family vacationed in the Great Smoky Mountains, Tennessee. I took three grandchildren, ranging in age from 6 to 12, into the forest to acquaint them with their spiritual selves.

I asked the children to touch various plants I pointed out and then tell me what each plant was used for and how it was to be applied to a person. This is the only instruction I gave, although none of the children had any previous experience doing this.

Each child responded without hesitation and told me exactly what their assigned plants could be used for, with all the particulars. Later on, I successfully re-peated this process with them before returning to our cabin.

Activating Divine Love Energy in Water

Their comments were 100% accurate. You see, children can use their intuitive spiritual skills even at a young age unless they are conditioned to conform to the thoughts and limitations imposed by adults.

You can learn to use your spiritual intention if you allow yourself to do so.

Chapter 8

Drug Addiction and Alzheimer's Programs

Drug Addiction Program

In the spring of 2017, we initiated a free spiritual research project to help people addicted to drugs. As reported in my previous book, DYNAMIC REALITIES AND DIVINE LOVE HEALING, the results of that Program were outstanding. Much of that book may be helpful in your life. Let's review the pertinent information.

Activating Divine Love Energy in Water

Anyone following the news today is aware that the addiction problem is severe and has too few rehabilitation successes. There has also been an exponential increase in drug abuse-related deaths.

We began the spiritual research program in March 2017 using the Advanced Protocol described in the book DYNAMIC REALITIES AND DIVINE LOVE HEALING. The Advanced Protocol worked well for people who truly wished to become well.

Some findings from the Drug Addiction Program:

1. People who wanted to release their addictions and were willing to let the Creator help them, recovered in approximately one week with no withdrawal symptoms. The chemical need for drugs was removed, and they had no further physical desire for drugs.

A Worldwide Healing Solution

2. People who did not believe in the Creator and those who were not sincerely interested in recovery did not experience any changes.

3. This spiritual research Program for drug addiction revealed to participants that the interaction between the spiritual realm and the physical realm is real and will be supported when people ask for and are willing to accept help.

4. In discussing the future of the Program with healthcare professionals, we determined that it would be difficult to introduce this full-scale healing Program in the United States due to our insufficient resources. The general public and local governments are primarily focused on expanding traditional recovery centers, even though such centers have low success rates.

5.Therefore, we asked the Creator to run the Program from the spiritual realm, in the mass consciousness energy field. This energy field surrounds the earth and serves as a storage location for spiritual intention programs; these programs can be accessed and used by spiritual persons.

The mass consciousness field cannot be manipulated by man and is under the direction of the Creator's Angels. (If you need clarification of this concept, please click on the Consciousness menu tab on our website for a comprehensive webinar on the mass consciousness. Or read the explanation given in my book, BEING AT ONE WITH THE DIVINE.)

6. One of the benefits of running this program from the spiritual realm is to accommodate even those who do not have access to our books or videos.

Today, people everywhere can be helped, provided their intentions are sincere, and they request Divine Love assistance from the Creator. People are automatically enrolled in the Program when they ask the Creator for help; they do not need to study or say a Healing Statement. Refer to our website for more information at: https://www.worldserviceinstitute.org.

The Alzheimer's Program

In 2017, we conducted another spiritual research Program. The Alzheimer's Program is intended to help people with advanced dementia and confirmed cases of Alzheimer's. What we learned was quite surprising.

If they lived at home, people with mild dementia rapidly recovered cognitive function. However, people in care facilities with secure Alzheimer's wards were generally non-responsive.

We learned that when family members visited their relatives in secure wards, they typically observed calm and serene patients. This usually resulted from the antipsychotic medications that had been administered to the patients. For this reason, we could not rely on reports from family members to evaluate a patient's condition.

When we asked the Creator to also run this Program from the spiritual realm, we learned that some people who asked for healing would be helped, but that others were not to be healed, for reasons known only to the Creator. Perhaps the Creator wants mankind to investigate and develop solutions related to the exact causes of Alzheimer's.

Once again, we accepted this spiritual guidance because of the significant number of unknowns. As with the Addiction Program, the patient's spiritual intent is the key to joining the Alzheimer's Program. Refer to our website for further clarification.

Chapter 9

Problems Facing Humanity

Many Choices, Many Problems

Our spiritual research healing experiences with Divine Love have resulted in significant recoveries for people who applied our Advanced Protocol and recognized the importance of changing their lifestyles. Yet, some people do not realize the need to do that, so they remain ill because of poor nutrition,

Activating Divine Love Energy in Water

unhealthy environments, and/or unhealthy relationships.

The overwhelming amount of information
available on the Internet and through
social media can make sound decision-
making difficult. People struggle to find
mental solutions to life problems rather
than surrender control to the Creator and
abide by the guidance they receive.
People fail to grasp this reality until they
have developed some working experience with our Advanced Protocol.

Also, some individuals with access to our
information do not allow enough time to
study the material. Those people who do
embrace Divine Love spiritual healing
learn how to achieve complete alignment
with the Creator and experience lives
with better health and greater happiness.

Throughout the world, people are over-
whelmed by chaotic events that have no
straightforward mental solutions. In this

chapter, we explore some of these issues and learn how we can work together towards solutions.

Meeting Health Demands

All over the world are health problems for which there are limited solutions or no solutions at all. In recent years, the media has reported increasing outbreaks of Ebola, cholera, and a variety of other illnesses produced from exposure to parasites, fungus, bacteria, viruses, chemicals, or radiation.

As stated in an earlier chapter, many countries lack sufficient doctors, medicines, or the means to distribute services rapidly to cope with these overwhelming problems. And many countries have restrictive healthcare laws limiting what is approved as treatment for a particular illness.

Unfortunately, it is impossible to keep up with the demand for solutions to such problems. Good science and safe manufacturing practices for pharmaceutical grade drugs require evidence-based, double-blind studies to determine the efficacy of new products.

Although most individuals suffering from debilitating or life-threatening diseases may not want to be part of double-blind studies, they do want access to available survival options, although often those options are experimental.

Worldwide Sharing of Healthcare Treatments

There seem to be few ways to share healthcare solutions globally. Some European nations have developed electronic equipment and medicines to treat a variety of diseases. While some of

A Worldwide Healing Solution

these have been accepted in the country of origin and elsewhere, others have not.

Electronic devices often represent too significant a deviation from existing treatment regimens. Electronic devices are used to stimulate the energy in the body with energy waves generated by these machines. Some machines are more effective than others, but most seem to have a beneficial effect.

Limited mindsets can stifle research and prevent viable solutions from being implemented.

In the Far East, healthcare is often based upon the application of herbs, diet, nutrition, acupuncture, and Chinese energy medicine, together with some drugs and modalities of other countries. The techniques offered through Chinese medicine, in particular, are profound and generally successful.

Activating Divine Love Energy in Water

Yet those same techniques have not been widely received in most Western countries. Similarly, laws in the Far East often restrict the wide-scale importation of the medicines and energy devices of other countries. Acceptance and rejection vary due to the vast differences between Eastern and Western approaches to medicine.

Much of Western medicine treatment relies upon the prescribing of drugs that have been developed through pharmaceutical company research. Those same medicines can interact with the remnants of medicines or other toxins that may have been stored in the body of a patient for many years. Interaction can lead to "side effects," which can cause unexpected interruptions to health recovery.

Over thousands of years, Eastern medicine has evolved healing solutions based upon energy effects rather than chemistry. Eastern doctors understand that

A Worldwide Healing Solution

every component of the human body, be it organs, tissues, blood, bone, nerves or muscles, emits different and individual energy frequencies.

Eastern doctors accept that herbs can be used for healing. The energy of those herbs is unique, and some herbs can be assigned to specific health problems.

Eastern doctors also think in terms of energy waves interacting with the energy fields of the human body. They often do not focus on a specific disease, but rather provide solutions to strengthen the human immune system. A healthy immune system can help correct or minimize detrimental effects in the body.

Because they think in terms of energy, Eastern medical researchers willingly investigate mechanical devices and electronic devices developed abroad.

Activating Divine Love Energy in Water

One problem observed in both Eastern and Western medicine is that it can take a long time to restore a damaged human immune system. Yet, once the human body is back in balance, the immune system can successfully cope with most illnesses.

In Western medicine, radiation, surgery, and medicines are expected to produce benefits faster and prolong life. Yet frequently when a procedure is done, the resulting long-term side effects inhibit the restoration of the immune system.

This is not the fault of physicians or the developers of medicines except in clear cases of misuse. Despite efforts to study drug interactions, it is virtually impossible to identify every single chemical buildup that exists in the body.

I noticed a curious thing about medical research databases. The reports appear to focus on short-term side effects up to five years from the completion of treatment. There is little data correlating the side effects that happen beyond five years.

Each patient usually has a complex medical record containing many potential drug interactions. Consequently, as medicines are applied, unexpected re-actions can begin to manifest beyond five years, with people developing additional severe, and/or life-threatening health problems.

Which do you prefer, Eastern or Western medicine? I believe that both systems have much to offer and that Divine Love healing can bridge any gap between them. Divine Love healing can also help increase positive patient outcomes and minimize side effects.

I look forward to a future where patients are offered more fully integrated global healthcare solutions without concern for cost, availability, or limited benefits.

Antibiotic Overuse

Another significant worldwide problem is antibiotic overuse. For many years, China and other countries have given antibiotics to animals for weight gain and health preservation.

Unfortunately, with continued use of an antibiotic, the targeted bacteria may eventually develop a resistance to that antibiotic. In the case of farm animals, some medicines have become ineffective.

On April 20, 2019, a fascinating program on the 60 Minutes television program showed how E. coli bacteria quickly mutated in the presence of a popular antibiotic, rendering that antibiotic useless.

A Worldwide Healing Solution

Some antibiotics are no longer effective in humans who have eaten treated animals. The mutated bacteria may have been transferred to humans from the animals, or the bacteria may have mutated in humans because of personal antibiotic overuse. For example, when a physician prescribes a standard antibiotic to combat a minor infection, something that would usually respond to the medicine, that antibiotic could be ineffective.

Some countries have only one or two antibiotics that work; others no longer have anything in their antibiotic arsenals that work. This means that highly infectious and rapidly spreading bacteria such as MRSA can become much more challenging to treat.

The future will likely see more brand-new diseases that are the result of bacteria mutations.

Chapter 10

All Living Things

This book has focused primarily on human needs, yet underlying many problems in the world is the fact that people have abused and ignored nature and its other inhabitants. Some species on Earth are nearly extinct because they have been over-hunted, poisoned, or deprived of food sources.

Fish harvested for human consumption have become a focus of consumer safety because many species contain heavy metal toxins such as mercury. Various fishing waters have been declared off-limits because of over-fishing or chemical contamination.

Trees and other plants are essential to life because they convert carbon dioxide into oxygen. The practice of stripping trees in the Amazon Delta of South America upsets the ecological balance of the Earth.

Plastics, municipal waste, and industrial waste in many countries have been indiscriminately dumped into waterways. This has caused an ecological problem that is reflected in the spreading of viruses and the near extinction of many fish and mammals. Most of the seas of the world are now contaminated with bacterial, viral, and chemical products.

On land, toxic chemicals have been injected into deep wells with the expectation that the hard rock will contain the chemical toxins for eternity. Yet, fractures in the Earth's strata are allowing liquids and vapors to escape containment areas and enter aquifers, which then become contaminated.

Because some countries allow hunters and poachers to operate indiscriminately, we will continue to see a decline in wildlife numbers. And when we continue to strip land for minerals and real estate, animal food sources disappear, along with the animals themselves.

It is doubtful that mankind will change behavior until a spiritual basis is adopted that causes us to become aware of the consequences of our actions. *Through the second petition of the Worldwide Healing Solution each individual's inner spirit will become aware of all the issues affecting them.*

The Creator has given us free will to decide if we want to create a heaven on

A Worldwide Healing Solution

Earth by acting responsibly. Someone who tosses trash from a car window only contributes to the problem.

What can you do to help? Share the Worldwide Healing Solution and its two Petitions with relatives, friends, and fellow workers.

As the Divine Love energy of the water systems in the world increases, our reality and environment can be altered to protect humanity and all living life forms. Toxins will become energetically neutralized.

We are all spiritual brothers and sisters of the same father we call the Creator or God. Do not be afraid; the Creator is in charge. We are witnessing a new reality that links the spiritual nature of mankind directly to the Creator.

We have already received reports of source water correction in rivers and

Activating Divine Love Energy in Water

wells and improvements in people's
health.

Please send me an email to:
healinghelp@worldserviceinstitute.org

Describe your personal observations as
you witness improvements in your environment and yourself.

Chapter 11

Measuring Energy

The measurement of energy can be straightforward, and various measurement devices exist, although some can be quite expensive.

However, once you realize that your true self (your inner spirit) will never lie to you, your spirit enables you to measure whatever you want, to whatever level you want. My previous book, DYNAMIC REALITIES AND DIVINE LOVE HEALING, gave examples for evaluating various food supplements and other consumables.

I recommend two simple methods of measuring energy. The first method requires that you *allow yourself to feel* the energy. Everyone has an energy field that radiates in space. Gain experience by using your open hand or your fingers and your spiritual intention to measure the energy field emitting from your own body or another person's body without actually touching the body.

The second method of measuring is *dousing*. It's been more than 30 years since I first trained people in the use of dousing wires to measure energy fields.

The Use of Dousing Wires

When I first witnessed dousing wires used to measure energy fields, I thought it was a trick! Since then, I have come to respect the technique. Dousing wires provide visual confirmation to help us understand what is being measured, with repeatable results.

Anyone can learn to use dousing wires. Dousing wires are useful to measure the energy fields of man without expensive equipment. Professional dowsers can locate underground water supplies with great accuracy.

A sensitive person can detect energy using nothing more than his hands or dousing wires. By stating the desired position of dousing wire deflections, the wires will show the outer edge of an energy field.

Build Your Dousing Wires

You can even construct your own dousing wires from ordinary wire coat hangers!

Activating Divine Love Energy in Water

Prepare two wire coat hangers: cut each hanger to be 16 inches on the long side and 4 inches on the short side. Bend each wire into an "L" shape, forming a 90 degree angle.

For a "deluxe" set of dousing wires, loosely cover the short side of each wire with a plastic sleeve so that the dousing wire can move without binding when held in your hand. The plastic sleeve may be held in place with a threaded nut.

The Principle of Dousing Wires

Thought is an energy field that can be used like a computer to measure other unseen energy fields. When you inhale and hold your breath, you power your thought/energy field.

To understand how *thought* works, think about how a computer functions. A computer has these key components:

A Worldwide Healing Solution

A *program* which the computer interprets and operates.

A *memory* which stores the program and other information to be worked upon.

A *processor* that calculates and directs information to a device that reports the result.

An *output device* that displays the results to us on something that we can see, such as a printer, a TV screen, or other instruments.

A *source of power* that drives the computer via a battery or your household electric power.

Similarly, in terms of your energy fields:

Your brain generates an idea, or *thought*, which is your *program*.

You transfer that thought to the dousing wires as an *energized memory system*.

Your body acts as a *processor*.

The dousing wires are both the *output device and the instrument display*.

You supply *power* from your energy field.

Using Dousing Wires

Hold a dousing wire lightly in each hand, as shown on the next page. Do not grip the dousing wires too tightly. Allow them to rest gently in the crease where your fingers join your hand. To give the wires more support, balance the short end of the dousing wire on the inside of your little finger.

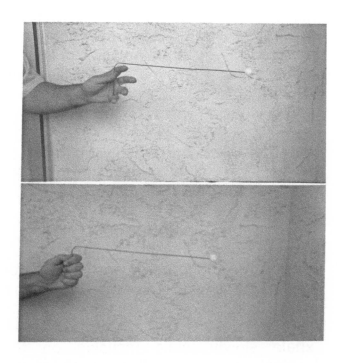

Activating Divine Love Energy in Water

Someone who is ill or energy depleted can pull the charge from *your* body when your energy field interacts with theirs. This is true whether you're holding dousing wires or not. However, by withholding your breath, you avoid having the energy charge pulled from you, especially when measuring someone's field with your hand or dousing wires.

Hold the wires horizontally (parallel to the ground) at all times during ANY measurement; do not tip them.

Inhale deeply, then hold your breath.

Develop the thought you wish to use for measurement, such as "measure Ann's energy fields."

Exhale slowly while focusing on the dousing wire tips. (This positions the thought about Ann at the outward tip of the wires.)

Inhale again, then hold your breath.

Watch the wire tips. Move slowly toward Ann until the wires deflect.

Note the position of the wires.

To disconnect from the measurement, pulse your breath lightly and lower the wires.

Understanding Wire Effects

As you begin walking forward, point the wires towards Ann. Ann's energy field will generally be radiating in space unless it has collapsed from a severe illness.

As you reach the outer boundary of Ann's energy field, both wires will move from pointing toward Ann to a position at right angles to your forearms. Each wire tip will be pointing away from your hands. When Ann is balanced energetically, this

Activating Divine Love Energy in Water

will be the desired and normal dousing wire position. See below. (Note that the balls at the end of the wires are not needed; they simply emphasize wire position for the photo.)

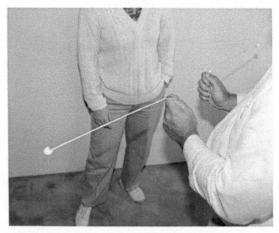

By standing in front of her, you can scan Ann's entire body without touching her. Lift the dousing wires vertically toward her head and lower them vertically toward her feet while holding the wires parallel to the ground at all times.

If Ann is not balanced energetically, one

or both wires will point to her disturbed energy field as you approach the troubled area as shown below.

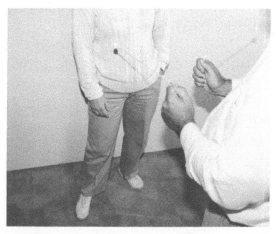

If this occurs, you should investigate further. Have Ann turn 90 degrees to her left so that you are now measuring Ann's right side. Watch the wires.

If the problem is on the right side, one or more dousing wires will point toward Ann's problem area. If you do not get a deflection after scanning up and down, have Ann face the opposite direction.

Activating Divine Love Energy in Water

Now you will be measuring Ann's left side. Again, if there is a problem, you can pinpoint the troubled area exactly with the dousing wires as you scan up and down her body.

Suppose Ann is standing sideways to you with her right shoulder facing you. You see that your left-hand wire points to your left and perpendicular to your forearm. But your right-hand wire points directly at Ann. This means that the energy problem is occurring on your right-hand side as you look at Ann's body.

Once Ann is energetically balanced using a Divine Love petition, her energy fields will be uniform; both dousing wires will be perpendicular to your forearms no matter what position on Ann you are measuring.

Other Dousing Measurements

With dousing, you can determine:

> The exact location of an energy program that is making a client ill.

> The location and status of the client's chakras (energy ports).

> Specific parts of the body that are blocking energy flow, which is helpful in cases of muscle weak ness or nerve damage.

> The exact location of radiation or chemical damage in the body.

> The location of the gland or organ exhibiting energy problems.

> Whether energy is leaking from a microwave oven.

The presence of a cosmic radiation shower in your neighborhood.

Precautions

People who are ill have a low energy charge in their bodies. When you approach them either with or without dousing wires, they can pull the energy charge from your body.

To avoid losing energy from your own body:

Always hold your breath as you measure client fields.

Always pulse your breath when you are finished to disconnect from your thought and measurement.

If you forget to hold your breath as you are measuring a client who is pulling charge from you, the dousing wire tips

A Worldwide Healing Solution

will probably cross over each other. To remedy this, pulse your breath, move away from the client, and re-balance your own body. Also, send Divine Love to the client as this will recharge his body.

Be aware that you may not be able to re-balance quickly after a massive energy drain. Use deep breathing for several minutes to recharge yourself if re-balancing your body is a problem.

Speed up re-balancing by holding the spiritual intention of taking in Divine Love and asking that your body be energetically balanced. You will feel the difference.

Always keep the wire tips several inches from the client's body. Be careful when you approach a client that the dousing wires do not swing toward his face, possibly striking him. Never touch the client with the dousing wires.

Practical Experiments

Have some fun with dousing wires. Go outside for this experiment: See if you can locate the water line that enters your home or apartment from the street. The dousing wires will open parallel to the direction of the pipeline.

Pour a glass of water to see whether you can measure the presence of the World-wide Healing Solution Petitions.

Be advised: *The Divine Love energy field you are measuring will radiate between 6 inches and 50 feet from your water sample.* The distance of the energy field of the Worldwide Healing Solution water will vary depending upon what Divine Love needs to do in your local water to protect you.

A Worldwide Healing Solution

Thousands Have Lived Without Love, Not One Without Water.

~ W.H Auden

Lightning Source UK Ltd.
Milton Keynes UK
UKHW010228230819
348430UK00001B/7/P

9 780997 690521